Afterimage

Afterimage

Poems

BENJAMIN VOGT

STEPHEN F. AUSTIN STATE UNIVERSITY
NACOGDOCHES ★ TEXAS

Stephen F. Austin State University Press
P.O. Box 13007, SFA Station
Nacogdoches, TX   75962-3007
sfasu.edu/sfapress
sfapress@sfasu.edu

Cover Art: Benjamin Vogt
Cover design: Laura Davis
Book Design: Brittany O'Sullivan
Manufactured in the United States of America

LIBRARY OF CONGRESS IN PUBLICATION DATA
Vogt, Benjamin
Afterimage / Benjamin Vogt
p. cm.
ISBN: 978-1-936205-57-8

1. Poetry. 2. American Poetry 3. Benjamin Vogt

ALSO BY BENJAMIN VOGT

Without Such Absence

Indelible Marks

Acknowledgments

Adirondack Review: "Indelible Marks" and "Pre-Elegy to My Mother"

Allegheny Review: "Minneapolis" (under "Indian Man")

Alsop Review: "Boy's Quartet—1949"

American Life in Poetry: "Grandpa Anderson's—1959"

Chanhassen Villager: "Lotus Lake, Minnesota"

Cream City Review: "A Suburban Affair"

Diagram: "My Father Visits the Homeplace," "Compatible," * and "An Evening Porch"

Ellipsis: "Loving Apparitions on High Street" *

The Evansville Review: "Fishing"

Ginger Hill: "The Whale"

Harpur Palate: "All That Was Said About the Korean War"

Hayden's Ferry Review: "Little Deep Creek—Oklahoma, 1984" *

Litchfield Review: "Photo of Grandpa and 155mm Howitzer—Korea, 1953" *

Permafrost: "Photograph of Chevy Axle and Wheels—1953"

Portland Review: "Still Life Refracted"

Puerto del Sol: "Suddenly Autumn" *

Quiddity: "Wichita, 1938" and "Family Reunion—Photograph, 1962"

Rock River Times: "Planting"

Segue: "Rising Up From Mulberry Street"

Southern Indiana Review: "Sundays—Clinton, OK"

Subtropics: "A Geologist's Love"

Valparaiso Poetry Review: "Uncle with Landscape—Kansas, 1954"

Verse Daily and *Wind Magazine*: "Section 117, Plot 21"

"Uncle with Landscape—Kansas, 1954" appears in *Red, White and Blues: Poets on the Promise of America* (University of Iowa Press);

"Compatible" appears in *Diagram.2: The Second Print Anthology* (Del Sol Press); "Japanese Garden" appears in *Breathe: 101 Contemporary Odes* (C&R Press).

Several poems were included in the chapbooks *Without Such Absence* (Finishing Line Press, 2010) and *Indelible Marks* (Pudding House, 2004).

"A Geologist's Love," "Retirement," "Grandpa Anderson's—1959," and "Photograph, 1990" received awards from the Dorothy Sargent Rosenberg Memorial Fund.

"Section 117, Plot 21" won the Joy Bale Boone Prize from *Wind Magazine*.

"Portraiture at Blanks' Photography—Weatherford, OK, 1978" was nominated for the *Best New Poets 2008* anthology by *Poemeleon*

* Nominated for a Pushcart Prize

For all the memories we've forgotten to capture.

CONTENTS

II.

III.

Three Photos That Define Me

1.

On Interstate 40, between Oklahoma City
and Weatherford, is the El Reno prison.
On the shoulder of the westbound lanes
a sign warns that hitchhikers may be
escaping convicts. A gray shirt lies flattened
on the white line of the highway.

2.

In a recently plowed-under wheat field
in the middle of Custer county
cows have been grazing on the bent
stalks of butter-colored wheat.
A little girl comes walking from the field
covered in brown and green feces.

3.

In front of a 50s teal-green rambler
a family stands next to a 1984 Jaguar XJ6.
One child wears a Pepsi sweater, leans away
from grandma's goodbye kisses; with arms
clasped tightly and heels against the tire,
someone's hand is coming down on his shoulder.

I.

The force of photographic images comes from their being material realities in their own right, richly informative deposits left in the wake of whatever emitted them, potent means for turning the tables on reality—for turning it into a shadow. Images are more real than anyone could have supposed.

—Susan Sontag, "The Image-World"

Photograph, 1990

Before construction started my parents put
a blueprint on the kitchen table asking me
which room I'd like. Then my father fashioned
three sets of miniature ceilings out of cardboard—
using an x-acto knife to make the angles—
and with my back against a wall he placed
them one by one above my head like half
formed continental hats I'd made in grade school.
Beneath each one I saw what it'd be like
lying awake at night on my bed, mapping out
the contours of the house that would protect
and then cast me out to a world of eight foot
ceilings flat and lacking this affection.
He said I had my choice since I was older
than my sister. It was the first time, twelve
years old and wanting to follow him, I saw
the architecture of my thoughts in form.
I felt the smooth lines above me as I reached
toward them, I felt the warmth of breath
and the heat of my face nuzzled in the safe
enclosure of that space. I felt the perfect shape
we made and see it now, again, through half
covered bones and missing doors, tall masts
of two by fours as scaffolding across
the sidewalk. I see the corner of that window,
set back and rising on the sill of one in front,
pushing light into the shadow of my home.

A Suburban Affair

Men move through car engines on Saturdays,
replace the wailing fan belts and clean

brand new spark plugs. Their ash-colored hands
fall and rise like tree lines in the wind.

At mid-day the push of sunlight into
the house's crevice shifts its weight

from thinning clouds, then draws out
the buried people. Grandmothers stir

like leaves to lawn chairs, nurse their walk
beneath the shade of eaves. Young men

play the driveway in one-on-one b-ball,
loop their bodies to the hoop like bows.

By afternoon the fire department is flushing
hydrants so the street moves smooth

like the Mississippi. Kids slide down the asphalt
in plastic sleds and tip their siblings on the cool curb.

In the black evening fathers grow into their
wives' embrace on porches and wait for

the night to become too dark—when the women
can't see their own hands reaching into another's,

like planting tulip bulbs above the roots
of suddenly still birches.

Lotus Lake, Minnesota

There on the north side where lilies grow out
in waves one-hundred feet thick, where the shallow

bottom surfaces in spring snow, a wooden dock lurches
forward from the thicket. Its dozen slips twist, turn

away from soil and itself, so it leans like a weathered
farmhouse in a field. It doesn't complain about

its disease, creaks are rare, it speaks only to fish and not
to bare footsteps of little girls in lime-green swimsuits,

or to the beat of sleepy men coming to fish the big one
soon after sun has shed night. I know it wants to argue

with boats and lilies and men. I know the winter ice
which strangled it is just as bad as the lake that so fast

is pulling it into itself. And we maybe, for a little while,
will use it too, standing above ourselves in the shimmer

of water, our hands and bones contorting like ghosts
slammed
into wooden pillars, sliding down along them to the
bottom

diving cool and dark into soil we cannot breathe,
but which, just as deliberately, pulls us in.

Uncle with Landscape—Kansas, 1954

The corner of the farmhouse, worn by wind
that has warmed fields for centuries, is bent
and sullied to the color clouds will carry

in April. Spades and rusted buckets lean
against a toppled silo, rows of wheat—
still green like lawns—converge, a vortex

of earth that's bent, retrieved by pausing light.
A boy is standing, six or seven, hands
in overalls and hair shaved army thin.

His teeth are white as Sunday shoes,
clean arms not yet tanned by earth or grease.
His glance, below center, turns away from sun

towards ground as if the day's not possible;
that on some lost acre, black and white
photo in grandma's album, he's become

the lines of fields, the sway of thinning wheat,
the passing shadow, brief and cloudless night.

Boy's Quartet—1949

It seemed our voices, just young enough to carry
        the echo of our parents' household
German, should've been enough to rouse
the men whose folded hands still shook with the fine
        patina of red clay fields. Perhaps the baby's
squawking would be subdued, unconsciously,
just long enough to bear our rhythm's call.

The schoolhouse room was filled with tired bodies
aching in the wood seats and bobbing dizzily,
        like heavy driftwood sifting through a river.
Our parents worked the land so hard, both here
        and in the old country, we felt a sudden
debt to remind them of what they risked and why.

Maybe all we had to sing was Schiller.
        But we stirred
them to their feet with the Star Spangled Banner—
        Miss Hutchins took her cue, began tilting
the classroom flag and pole behind us, pulling
it back and forth like a railroad switch plate.

Men from the war stood like rusted windmills, firm
        across the field of women's bowed heads.
Kids glanced from one to another unsure of what
they could get away with in all this indirect
attention. But we sang with bravado—roosters
        waking the insides of a farm house—puffed
our chests, straightened our thin arms, let voices

dishevel the spirits of a hungry audience.
We took them into the rows of wheat and Chevys
        lined around the old schoolhouse, the marriages,
appointments, loaves of sweet bread in the oven.

At eighteen it seemed right to ask, if anyone
        could see America superimposed
with stars and stripes over the swinging
        front doors, the wheat, the baggy
pants of lean old men prodding cattle to the pen,
the everyday movement we lost ourselves in—
        if we were still worth anything, if fate
would save us for something grander than tonight.

Wichita, 1936

Who are we standing by the house's shadow,
linking our own with chestnut trees that wear
the stone foundation, uprooting all we know?

Our Sunday best beneath the flimsy portico
makes ma and pa like stalwart marble pillars.
Who are we standing by the house's shadow?

This morning wind rolled up the calico
fields, dust and bean sprouts purred through air
uprooting the foundation of what we know

behind our house. Pa laid his hand on the window,
each finger strong as a bridge crossing rivers,
linking fields beneath our house's shadow.

The sun shoots through the warping walls like arrows
though none comes close to me. The quiet bears
our stone foundation rooting what we know.

Most days our hands are not enough. And though
we'll pass them on, reform them through the earth,
we're always standing in the house's shadow—
a stone foundation uprooting what we know.

Mildred, Two Fords, and Her Friends at 16—1938

That's Caitlyn, always smelled like stew,
but Caitlyn got the boys—it's true
that love first enters through the nose.
Margorie spoke often of her woes:
the custom shoes that came too late
from New York for Sunday dates
just after church, or flowers freshly
placed by her maids—incorrectly.
Janey got lost in fields of wheat
that paralleled the only street
to town. Her father often rode
the tractor up and down the windbreaks,
calling out for her mother's sake.
Florence stayed at home most evenings,
coaxed out only to go fishing
or wander toward the Indian mounds—
the silence of these places found
a better friend than others could.
And then Denise who chopped our wood
in winter, fixed axles in summer,
steered clear of trivial wonder:
she wanted chores that had results,
and never kept from telling insults
if they made you buck up, move on.
And there was me, I'm second
from the right. But it's just a blur—
who I was, the girls, the sudden stir
of dust-filled shadows on these roads.

Rural Kiss—Oklahoma, 1944

Because she's saying her goodbyes, your bodies
writhe like clothesline shirts, the briefest touch
felt deeper than her coat's arm like the clutch
of Chevy parked behind, its chrome a frieze
which cools her arching back. You push valise
away like an airplane's wheel block, insomuch
to steady your expressions—hers in such
untangled wonder and lusty indices.
But yours is black and white, eyes open, a search
for something past her curling hair, which fades
the house, the drive, street sloped and glistening.
Today avoids you, your memory a perch
from which a distant and voiceless sound invades—
without the war all love is just routine.

High School Mixer—1956

He's clearly used to something else—not girls,
that's brutally clear. Your hand is placed awkward—
palm facing toward the middle of your bodies,
thumb dangling lost outside the grasp.
His body's stiff, though you look up
into his eyes directing him—he doesn't
notice anything but the dim light, flash bulbs,
music he can barely step to. No belt.
He doesn't even have a belt, and his shirt
is coming untucked. Your dress, a layered fluff
of white with a black strap around the waist—
you could lend it to him, the thin-laced belt
that ornaments your slender hips. His hand
is placed right there, just above your side.
If his fingers slid a little more, if thumb
could saddle in, hide from all the other guys
and lights and sliding shoes across the floor,
if any part of him could find its way
to you and rest awhile—oh what a fine
evening it would be, what a man he'd be.

Wedding—June 9, 1958

A simple dress, off white, but enough
to bring you to love's door step and the eyes
of the man beside you. He's in his army dress:
one silver medal on his chest and a father's
cufflinks, medals too, against the army green.
He's worked a smile toward the ceiling, forced
straight his left arm like a fence post. But you've
clasped his right so tight it's bent awkwardly
as you scoop the locked hands against your hip.
You smile to the right, pass his sightline,
two deer-eyed glances crossing maybe six
feet out in front where older women smile,
slightly turn their heads in toward the aisle,
while their husbands focus straight ahead.

Photograph of Chevy Axle and Wheels—1953

Someone said they parked it there just to see
what would happen when the train came
down from KC. They knew that here, in the middle
of fields that only sparrows kept, the train
would be coming fast: far enough from beginning
to be moving hot and hungry for somewhere else.

This wasn't like that time the milkman swung
the County 7 curve too harsh, his heavy pendulum
of jugs and bottles carrying him late for 5am—
this wasn't just an accident. The truck sat across
the rails out of simple country curiosity.
It's all gravestones now.

An axle here. A tire there. Driver's door scooped
and torn like drugstore ice cream curled
inside the spoon. Metal on metal is much more
permanent. But if someone left, and lost themselves
along this railway, no one would pay it much attention.
No one remembers unless they have a souvenir.

Only flesh on flesh made the family scrapbooks.
For years the kids strolled along the place and dug
for bolts, glass shards, mementos of cool. Now
fields slide over ties like passing clouds, uninterrupted.
Sparrow shadows dip into wheat and come out whole—
reminders of what's become and what is gone.

Grandpa Anderson's—1959

The food is on the table. Turkey tanned
to a cowboy boot luster, potatoes mashed
and mounded in a bowl whose lip is lined
with blue flowers linked by grey vines faded
from washing. Everyone's heads have turned
to elongate the table's view—a last supper twisted
toward a horizon where the Christmas tree, crowned
by a window, sets into itself half inclined.
Each belly cries. Each pair of eyes admonished
by Aunt Photographer. Look up. You're wined
and dined for the older folks who've pined
to see your faces, your lives, lightly framed
in this moment's flash. Parents are moved,
press their children's heads up from the table,
hide their hunger by rubbing lightly wrinkled
hands atop their laps. They'll hold the image
as long as need be, seconds away from grace.

Family Reunion—1962

Christine is doing Jane's curls in the dark.
It's dark except for the fuzz against the wall
where projector light diffuses to eggshell white—
an image of Jane doing her own hair at five

on the trip to Grandma's farm near Wichita.
Thank God, she says, *you have on clothes today.*
Her mom shushes her for swearing. Laughing
behind the cover of hair and brush, Christine
whispers, Jane laughs, the slides go on.

Christine's proud uncle shows the family archive
he's worked on for the last four years. They have
to be polite. This is history. His story, too.
With yawns in concert with the click of every slide
jaws clasp shut as quickly as they can,

but echo the monotone of light and time.
Oh Jane, Christine thinks to herself. *Oh Jane*
we mustn't stay here any longer. The roads
are there just out the door and the fields—
they're moonlit walls and all we'll ever know.

My Father Visits the Homeplace

It's not the porch that keeps you to yourself,
the splintered sun-worn posts analogous
to how you see the countryside. Your sight
and silence bearing down above the fields
is from a center you don't know, in waiting
you can't get closer to it. Do you feel
the maple lifting, slightly, in the breeze,
stretched on its toes to dance abruptly by
a father's sawdust breath? And do you touch
the morning glories with your backhand like
your mother's German cheek, whispering
go now to the dark which brought you here?
It's not the rows of warping banister
and deck that holds you back, but fields of skin
like grass, emblazoned in such bruising heat.

All That Was Said About the Korean War

In the summers my grandparents would spray
poison on the juniper in front of their house.

The tree would soak as bagworms, grown on
to branches like pine cones, dripped to the ground.

When I became too curious grandma would yell
to get out of the way, to move downwind

and avoid the mist. But from behind grandpa
I couldn't see a thing. His plaid shirt would

unfurl like loose sails around his gut, his heavy
arms bent and recoiled in the action like palm trees

under the rush of low-flying jets. From deep
in his shadow I could only sense the dying bugs,

the heavy-wet branches, the man with a cigarette
balancing from his mouth like flesh.

That sweet air cut through my lungs like chlorine,
glued to my mind so that today, standing in the shower,

I understand there's nothing in the world
to protect me from dying, and that each year
the juniper now harbors every invasion.

Unemployed on a Summer Porch in Marysville, OH

It is nearly past evening and clouds spread
thin like smoke over houses. The radio says
rain is falling somewhere but you let
the voice fade in a sudden breeze which
erases, rephrases what you hear.

When you were a boy your mother sang
late-night lullabies you heard on television—
ads for Texas, Pan Am, Chevrolets.
You felt as if you were full of going,
as you do now, the lips of shirt sleeves
open like sails, yet moored to lawn chair.

It is almost dark and you can see
the break in clouds grown smaller, bruised
to purple then black. You've turned
the radio off, begun humming to yourself—
even nightingales are hiding their desire.

Section 117, Plot 21

This field, which weathers January warmth,
grows crows and sparrows by a hundredfold.
From under the bent stalks winged shadows rise,
harsh echoes stab the desert place before
the sky grows pointillist black. With bellies full
of hollow grain, they float through one another.
Their awkward cloud collides in distant voice
as each jackhammer beak looks down, surveys
the broken land then dives to take the combine's
once calculated route.

                The farthest rows
remain uncut. Their rotting guts hold fast
to wrapping-paper skin. This broken farmer,
whose bank has called his promissory bluff,
lies somewhere with his windows opened wide,
listening to distance. Clean hands lay folded
across his belly. Each breath lifts them slightly
higher to God. And when the empty roads
and barren trees allow the soundlessness
to come dive blindly through his house, he hears
the fields, his earth, splitting open as flocks
gorge themselves.

              He'll sell his father's Deere.
The spades as well. The home place, the Ford,
five hundred acres with the bass-filled lake—
and on Saturdays he'll cast his line into
his wife's herb garden. On his knees he'll claw

the rows and listen to his humming partner
who hovers over him, prepares the harvest.
The farthest field is slipping through his hands.

Portraiture at Blunks' Photography—Weatherford, OK, 1978

Her hand upon his chest like buttress, palm
in shallow rest between his tie and coat—
how its fingers curl just softly, pleading this
is not what's kept him on his feet. With him

beside her—thinner lips and whiter skin
and the gray like panhandle snow—
the months of rest, appointments, endless nights
refuse to linger in their steadfast smiles.

He's the husband, father of boys and land
and real estate, a dozen parcels west of town
where wind from two directions holds
the wheat erect, defiant. Where late

into the harvest night, he hears the shallow
whisper that all grown men refuse to hear.
Between the whirling thrush of dust and stalks
chipped by the combine—the time it takes

to re-approach from the distant lines of wheat—
he knows the summer night that cools his cheek
is just a careful prelude, patient push
into the friction of his aging body,

like stones pressed into a façade, the mortar

of earth and water loose against a stolid frame.
He knows that as the distant night's work
will go on until it's done—until the necessary

reaping of earth and months of dusting fields
and irrigation end—no stalk, no tree,
no God could hold him any nearer life
than the imprint of the morning's photograph,

the gentle hand still warm against his body.
He imagines, in the nearing lights of combine,
a careful way of leaving simply, without
the circling eyes, near whisper of machines

that pulse into his heart, without the thrush
of sudden memory piercing through the air.
He imagines, as the load of grain is siphoned
to the truck bed, how sudden form can falter—

how watching lifted fields now fall like rain,
that even a few firm stalks have made it past
as if threaded through the terror purposely,
released into the rush, become the silent whole.

Indelible Marks

God cannot give the rivers any more rain
and the riverbed stone breathes sky.

Oklahoma City is so very far away,
it is like a woman's mouth in wine.

The soil is red, the water is red,
the people come up from it white,

and all the whiskey and polished beads
will never make up for its lack.

One road outside Tulsa
moves south, double-ribbed.

Nothing moves. Wind no longer sees,
but is just shade in a mirage.

God cannot take you from this place
even after you have left it.

Weatherford, 1983

for M. V.

We take a walk outside in the August heat
where the peach tree is ready—heavy fruit
magenta on the sunny side, orange in the shade.
The bird fountain has a robin in its metallic,
green water, and the silk tulips, planted
by the garage, are still in bloom. She straightens
a plastic hair net on her perm before
helping my sister climb into the tire swing,
then gives a light push. Carpenter ants file
up the oak's trunk, across limbs, and down
the swing's rope to tickle our small hands.
I watch as she shakes white pellets from a box
at the base of the tree, each ant rushing
to carry their load. I can't help but feel
the weight they must have, making repeat trips
to offer the colony this bounty, this graceful act
of inevitable sorrow. My gratitude is for
the potato soup and zwieback later that day,
the onions and salt that make me cough
on the first spoonful, the sweet texture
of warm bread that chases it away.
But the memory of this turns the soup to tears
and the rolls to a lump in my throat.
How is it that nourishment becomes pain
before it becomes nourishment again?
That in order to live you must first lose?
Any moment may be the one we carry deep

into our lives, offer to our families again,
like sustenance, as we walk in August heat
where the tire is gone, but the tree thrives.

II.

The wheat leans back toward its own darkness,
And I lean toward mine.

— James Wright, "Beginning"

Itinerary

Again, you've bought my plane ticket.
You arranged my visit because you fear
we're losing touch, but you call and say
it's all arranged—and doesn't this feel
like losing touch? Too often you remember
and place *remember* down the road
so there's something to look forward to.
You and I leapfrog loss without touching
because two objects cannot occupy the same space.
All of this matters when you say, the day before,
how everything is perfectly prepared, the plan
with so much purpose I don't find love in it but
some wary treaty, a barter for our better parts.
We're becoming too human, slipping opposite
like sunrise and set at the same moment,
blobs of hidden divinity stumbling to orbits
that meet at some calculated time. Yet even
scientists aren't sure on this. The plane
may not land. It wouldn't be the first time.

Pre-Elegy to My Mother

1.

You must not die slowly like the hiss of logs
settling into a fireplace in January,
the water boiling from veins on to a blue flame.
You are like a well which brings up
a buried lake to irrigate the fields—a gravy
ladle reaching out over a plate, mashed
potatoes and the crater lakeshore forming,
the filling of space like nourishment and heat.

2.

You cannot live like this. No more than ice in July,
a picnic cup's dissected bits laid out
on the grass and asphalt drive—
the underbellies of cubes melting,
slicking a path down to the street and
backing into the space afraid. You are full
of the moment when you lied out in a lawn chair
and could smell a distant fire melting.

Rising Up from Mulberry Street

With window open, jayhawks belch
their search-sounds into rooms with
chenille sofas, leather wingbacks,
wood floors that roll the echo deep
from outer room to inner. It's as if some
memory of tree, now flat, stained
and polished, is still upright
in the minds of birds. They know
this house needs them from
the inside out, displaced like a locomotive
pawing through prairie, sky stuffed
with low gray clouds, metal caw off-pitch,
belly burning oak and maple incense.
They know the fiber of motion rests
in their communiqué, fills the hollow made
by closed doors, plaster walls, streets perched
in rolling miles of replicate splendor.

Faith

I can't explain it. If I could there'd be
grand illustrations of intense color,
the lack of blindness squinting into sunrise.
There'd be the sound of stillness,
which is not a sound but a flavor
like cold gulps of water in late July.

Sometimes the intensity of nothing
is like electrical wire pulled taut
through the bones of a house. No one
thinks of their existence behind drywall,
just that outlets and switches effect
some ethereal composition of a room.

When I entered the Lincoln Cathedral
there was a vacuum of sensation.
Coldness, sullenness, vacancy, a depth
of distance no mortal could extend through.
Yet the windows rainbowed through it as if light
pledged itself against the shadows we made.

Great Grandmother—1950

In your black dress—and not because of death,
but because your piety must shelter absence—
is this why priests and nuns wear shadows?

Your topmost button is a silver broach
that clamps your neckline like a bible verse:
thou shall not, parents used to begin, flesh

is the devil's mirror and man will shatter himself
to get inside. Even your hair, a tight
gray bun, gives no room for any man

who might still have a spark of man within—
you are always business, goddess, progenitor
of making nothing out of something. Atop

your house's concrete steps, between the shade
of roof and morning sun, you hold one arm
behind you while the other flattens pleats.

The power shrouded in your fist is equal only
to your squinting eyes, the focused dark of cloth,
the countless evenings anticipating daylight,

a half formed smile draped by wrinkles
closing toward forgiveness of the body.

Mothers Calming—1930

I said to hold the baby flat, to tuck
its head inside the elbow. Lean and rock,
don't flinch or twitch a muscle, girl.
Don't laugh or cry because your heart might shake
and overtake his own. He wails as he curls
against you. He feels the bonds you couldn't fake,
the stretching, grasping, heavy undertow
of obligation other than his wrestling body.
Darling, my child, my only child, you know
about such things. Even now through muddy
distance, two dozen years, we feel what's under
the other's skin and hold it slow, with wonder.

Fishing

I'll take the best part of you down to the lake,
past the honeysuckle scent on the south-side
of the house, back down the towering tree-god
hillside, falling like rivers of storm water
into the willow roots at the shoreline bottom.
I'll cast your soul out over the lily pads in June,
skip it along the smooth evening surface,
hit the pink reflections of the sunset behind
my hapless expressions. I'll let your soul sink
to the bottom, through the tumbling weeds,
waving breathless underneath the brown glass
that lets me see nothing too deep, nothing you'd
ever shown me. It's gone, that part of you,
hidden by summer smells of moss and lily, sunfish
schools racing to live a little while longer. And you
were worried about the car starting, or that quiet friend
who never came to you like me down low, by the shore,
looking out carelessly into our stunned reminiscence.

Sundays—Corn, OK

Today I will have to visit you.
It has been too long between trips
and I don't want you to say
in those first few minutes,
I wouldn't want to see me either or
I'm happy you're keeping so busy.
I will have to say then how good you look,
how you seem stronger, how surprised
I am that the birthday flowers haven't wilted.

You will ask if I want a drink, and I don't,
but you try to get it rolling over
the edge of the recliner.
So instead I open the fridge and two cans
of soda. Your mouth must be dry
after having said so much.

An hour later you will take your pills,
and I will watch the procession,
your throat contracting at each place
that I take for granted as I swallow
in exact sympathy. You look over at me, smile,
then look out the window as if you saw
something rise out of me and float
towards the sun. I will tell you goodbye.

That I will call soon.
You will watch me leave and you will
wave to my back. You will go to bed,

wake up and remember every day is the same
again. In boredom you will call me first.
In fatigue you will hang up first.

Some day you will remember holding me only once,
the night I was born; and so now, from every day on,
I stand long in the shower before bed
letting the steam and water find
the wrinkled grooves in my own skin,
lifting parts of me up from myself too,
until all the rivers meet like lost tributaries
at the edges of the drain.

Photo of Grandpa and 155mm Howitzer—Korea, 1953

for Robert Anderson

I'd have asked him.
       Grandma said he never
       talked about it. Not with her,
       not anyone, not
       even in his nightmares.
I'd have asked him.

Tell me a story of the winter
       ghosts you can't imagine.
Tell me something about the Chosin
       mountains that couldn't survive.
Tell me what you wrote in letters
       as your breath propelled the ink.

I'd have asked him who he killed,
       who died against him in a foxhole,
what the days meant when days
       meant nothing so much as warmth.

I'd have asked him to look me in the eyes,
       grab hold of my flimsy shoulders,
tell me even in the days before us there's
       a shadow that isn't cast by anything.

Waiting

With every call, each passing breath that rises
from shallow eyes, there is the weather settled
between us. Window daisies croon with motion,
the only sign of things beginning, scents
of spring that cover antiseptic wash.
There are machines that regulate our lives
together. Mountains of artificial air,
filtered from me to you. Occasional
interruptions delight us—language grown
so heavy nurses figure I'm less obligated
as afternoons transform to mornings, fear
of night akin to closing eyes. *It's sad,*
you look to me and say, *so obvious*
you're waiting for the perfect word to come.

Pilgrimage to Oaxaca, Mexico

Aurelia Aurora Catarino,
not a sunrise event
or a winter optical illusion,
though some might claim
she is a merchant of miracles.

Shaman, a *curandera*, a woman
who instills dream and vision
to the less fortunate. Salvia
Divinorum—her plant, a hallucinogen,
it shows what needs to be seen;

Not the villages in corn fields
or mushrooms and flora grown
along hillsides, but the God who
once dipped himself into creation
and left fields to grow untended.

The ceremony requires abstinence
from anything pleasurable, self-indulgent.
Only the trance can lead you from
the village of Huatla de Jimenez,
only fired leaves can smoke
you out of your fragile body,
image of the missing element.

The Whale

Thousands of Vietnamese are making pilgrimages
to a beach in southern Vietnam to worship a dead whale.
        — Associated Press

This is Darwin's fault. This is evolution's attempt
at developing the missing link. Or this is the spirit
of Jonah, indelible in the whale's mind, calling forth
the great beast to deliver him back to the shore.

No, this is happenstance. This isn't fate or faith.
This is an animal trying to capture prey by
pushing them against the beach, then sticking
to a sandbar unable to wrangle free. In this one place

the lack of a whale may mean a few more fish
in a few more nets. It may mean nothing more than
local architects securing work for a few days, building
bone shrines. Some lamps may shine brighter at night.

Some meals may be longer. But the coast will smell
worse than it normally does and the waves will punish
the whale until it fades into formlessness, then finally earth.
So in the end this is faith. This body giving up its reason.

Still Life Refracted

A company called LifeGem has begun taking
orders to create diamonds made from carbon
captured during cremations.
         — Associated Press

Your half-life has extended exponentially.
Now, instead of looking up to the near
and far spittle of stars—making up stories
for our children and memory—you can be cupped
river water, frozen, pressed into manageable shape.

Your pendent life, loose across my breast,
reminds me of rough elbows, concave
back, tomato smell of neck. I can finger
you even when you're not there, or here,
whatever this is. At night, lying in bed,
I can hold you up across flashlight,

rock our sleep in rhythmic trance mumbling
starlight, star bright, give me faith tonight.
I gather you, compact you in my soul, dream
you like sparkle dust in magic shows—transform
the body into something harder than love.

July, Just Outside Columbus

The fireflies are hovering over corn,
young fields darkened by maple shadows swept
across the dusk line. Beetle bodies pulse,
bright chemicals like breath released
into the body light the ground ahead,
as if a thousand searchlights were adrift.

Males are calling, their incandescent lust
an impatient spark, the female's waiting glow
a calm amongst this storm that binds desire
to action. Windows hover like dim suns while,
just fifty feet away, the fireflies are

like pens on paper, brief calligraphy
transposed to translucent night. Their body-light
a memory ongoing, dream of purpose
blown down to grass, then lifted up as if
a speckled hand were rising from the waters,
reformed like polished diamonds, cool and warm

against our momentary senses. How many
suns will rise and set on this frenzied hour,
work that the body needs between lost moments;
a bloodless still life when we clearly see
one-hundred lifetimes asking questions when

our mouths should have been more pensive, full
with speaking this silence—not ours, not theirs—

but meeting at a time and place where neither
are gods or creatures, one and the same light,
because we need the dark to find our way.

III.

Even here, even at the beginning of love,
her hand leaving his face makes
an image of departure

and they think
they are free to overlook
this sadness.

—Louise Glück, "The Garden"

Loving Apparitions on High Street

Streets that I had chanced upon, —
you had just walked down them and vanished.
— Rainer Maria Rilke

Even now, having given up and settled
for coffee on a portico above the sidewalk, every
perfume that rides the pull of air from passing cars
carves into me so smoothly I no longer mind but
enjoy the subtle pain. It's like toes curled beneath
a dancer who pirouettes, or hands warming beneath
the weight of a body—the pressure of some greater
presence so welcome that lesser displeasures
seem charming and necessary. Even religious men
speak of how darkness facilitates and augments light.
So when I think of you, our distance spreading
with a desirous elasticity, you're the light of shadows
in my memory. When I think of you it's essence
over matter. Even the city can't hold you near.

A Geologist's Love

There's no heat in her hands. No solace in her embrace.
      She presses herself into another so hard, she hopes
      the pressure fuses a center brighter than the sun.
      She says she wants to be mined like coal.

The cold metal scraping at her insides, methodical, each
      valley seismographed and core sampled, researched
      and then unearthed. She wants to be on display.
      She wants her inside breath to know the April rain.

Her heart to pump the clouds and rivers like her blood,
      to cleanse the storms and nightfall and mud
      until she can see through them toward the beginning.
      But the beginning, she's seen in books, was dust

and ash, sparkle radiation, plasma pools and sharp rock.
      Fragments of ice. Fog and daggers of creation.
      She says her bones are stalagmites sharpened
      beneath a dense ocean that drips onto her.

Irony, she says, is the morphous water sharpening the minerals,
      evaporating the cold smooth and leaving the element.
      She says she can offer nothing more than distilled parts
      constantly melting beneath the mantle of her skin.

Compatible

Are the trees and the interstates
among them? Jet planes in erratic
white cumulonimbus? Dandelions
in cracks of city sidewalks?

And you ask day after day what
these things mean, if black is not
really white, if it can ever be,
if lack is really intense fulfillment

and we—so focused on the shallow
pool of our language—just don't
recognize this joy. If you could
touch me right now, would you?

What if your body evacuated
into mine like a levee spilled
on the town? The difference
between reclamation and possession

is inundation. And you ask
if this is good or bad and I say
irony is sublime and leads
to transcendence. And you muse

on the spider behind your shades
that won't come out, your can
of poison ready to spill upon its
body, then scream and back away

once it reveals itself leg by leg—
its shadow more mercurial than desire.

Minneapolis

The obese Indian man
stands still before me
"full throttle" written
across his dirty t-shirt
beautiful women walk by
with long totem-pole legs smoking
hair rising out of their soul-
skinned bodies dreaming of his
destiny and of course they are
he knows by the thickness
of clouds and the temper
of fluttering birds and the beat
bouncing of the Aquatennial
tennis ball in July when
the harvest moon is near
full and his mother's womb
is empty long saddened by
his dislodging and apparent
lack of remembrance and thanks
still knowing but asking if he
does he know how beautiful he is

Aquatennial – Festival held in downtown Minneapolis, MN

After a Night Class at OSU

Everything is on a leash. Men on
cell phones calling home, bikes
hugging lampposts, ivy cut
back from brick buildings.

Most of us just want to go home,
be called, sung to, led through
shadows quickly. Some of us
will sit in cars with engines

idling, parking lot empty, feel
the body slip into something more
comfortable, melt into night
like Scioto driftwood or wind

broken between passing cars—
a momentary vacuum drawn tight
then released—stone-faced images
of lovers inside. Everyone trusts
the air to keep us where we are.

Awaiting the Performance of *Figaro*—Palace Theatre

Voices like hands puddle on my shoulder,
lap into my ear, become drunk with the echo
of themselves, this cascade of language dripping
tongue tip, ice hot pre-revelry—oh song, gentle force
that builds like fire, races up my spine as through
tinder wood, forest of longing reaching
to the heavens like bare bones exposed by wind,
the whole of the world spinning them dry and clean,
year upon year. And then the intermittent thrush
of bodies moving, bemoaning existence,
crashing on memory of what expectation is—
exaltation of the self, a profuse madness
that becomes intangible in the morning
when sun devours shadows, the calls
of a few leftover and inaudible tide pools—
promises and sweet nothings sunk
into the shallow recess of memory—pushed
below the tense surface, the feel of skin lost
against the music's sandy grain, the seductive
calls echoed between walls and slowly
diminished, the inevitable dispersion.
Oh voice that must turn away, oh body
that must travel far from me, oh soul
that must navigate this swallowed distance.

An Evening Porch

Just the sound of the monarch on lavender is.
    February snow across the fields
    and in that insulation of infinite
    space miles of silence carefully
    placed on every bare object.

Two of us are not one but an ocean of.
    Galaxies undulating
    hurricanes on satellite
    letters rising from the table
    in a sudden breeze.

Roads are something fearfully near as.
    Fires in the hills and
    yellow jackets in the eaves and
    any moment may be
    at any moment love.

Planting

for J.C.

Humidity has set the mood. A stillness
anticipating the brief evening shower, sudden
intoxication leashed to the earth. We wrestle
roots into dry soil before the cloudbank
shadows sunlight, before the dust turns to mud
and our hands become indecipherable
to this knowledge of flesh and bone, beginning
and end of the aching body. How the Penstemon
settles against the wall like a child
whose arms are folded to a pillow beneath
her head. And how the Coral Bells, with heavy
crimson leaves, pierce the garden air
with stalks of white blooms just larger than
a scattering of early season snowfall.
Already they are peaceful, understood.

And after earth washes from the bed's lip—
the sidewalk dark with water from the hose—
after black containers, shovels, labels
that tell us what will become and for how long,
after fatigue has quickly put it all away,
I realize I have never tasted earth
this deeply, felt its body warmer,
so swiftly placed an afternoon inside of me.

Fire Pit

The maple, a week ago bare,
bones honestly among us,
now covered in green,
shy in its
unconscious shadows.

It shifts, burns
like smoke seeking
out the air to heaven,
riding hand-currents
which brush aside

the cool spring night,
made warm by
dead limbs melting,
by bones giving up secrets.
I have held in my entire life.

Florigraphy

The Victorians had to be discreet about expressing their feelings toward one another since they were governed by strict moral codes of conduct. As a result, they used specific flowers and leaves to convey messages of adoration toward one another. These messages were often between young lovers inexperienced in romantic endeavors.

Having finally led her to a bench beneath a maple, I cautiously stutter and speak in the language I most trust. In my right hand I unfurl a sweet briar, my attempt to explain my wounding her, and my desire to patch our secret wounds. In my left is a fleur-de-lis so she knows I burn with love and uncontrolled confusion. She points across the path from whose hedge we gaze, and her trembling hand mimics the rapt fern in the breeze. I reach to her as a honeysuckle, but she withers like maple leaves in a flame—how could I have become her oleander? Her hair is like sage with perfect virtue, her lips sweet peas delicate and lingering. I stand up straight toward the sky as a multitude of oak leaves on stern limbs, find my way a few feet off to gather myself in narcissus. I feel her eyes follow me with brushes of trillium breath waiting, even pleading for the right word or action to bring us together. *Daffodil!* I finally cry. *I renounce all others. You are my iris, my compass star. Let us walk to the hyacinth so it will permeate our hearts. My thoughts of you are pansies and I cannot find unhappiness when they are of you. I am coreopsis when I dream of you. I pray you are like white clover when I must leave you, if even for a moment. My peony overwhelms my morning glory, and so I apologize earnestly.* She smiles broadly as our gazes lock, as if infinite and unbreakable arms, as if ivy on our wedding day. She bursts forth to me like primrose and daffodils—she has always been my hidden morning glory.

French Formal Garden

A oui, but you cannot look at me. You cannot come to me as just anyone. And not just anyone. Long live the king. You see, I am a gala event, an avenue in avenues in avenues of symmetry. Define me in your wide perpendicular strolls across crushed gravel, define me in diagonal shortcuts to the circular center where fountains blaze twenty meters high, crisscross, and tangle their long necks in intricate, angelic dance. I am pleasure and leisure. If you come out directly from the palace and stand atop the raised portico, you'll see I never end. Though the bosquets of poplar and cyprus along the flanks diminish both in number and size to the horizon, the vista of fields beyond are grand and still mine. The villages I acquired, too, the rivers moved aside into perfect canals, the town, Paris, the country, the world. I unfurl like wisdom and memory. It took eighteen thousand men to give me motion, their philosophies and religion my strolling narrative. They are mine, those men. They are parterres of low-cut boxwoods trimmed to patterns of elegant Venetian lace—a homage to my forebears, homage to the gondoliers hired from afar to sail my shallow pools so that I might grace them, too. Long live the king. And not just anyone. You cannot come to me as just anyone. You dare not look at me with ennui.

English Romantic Garden

Remember the mornings when we were children? The smell of
eggs fresh from the distant roost, the searching faith of sunlight
against our opening eyes, and those purple irises mother would
delicately place in a milk jar on the kitchen table? How far we've
come—and still we hunger for those young organic wilds; so we
find them transplanted here. If you visit in early morning, or even
in the mirrored late evening, the air is less agitated by the sun and
you can catch the same iris lining the stream. If you sneak into
the cool damp musk of the oaks and yews you can sit awhile as
my white jasmine and smoky blue wisteria replenish your spirit
like moonlight. There is something primal here, something to be
remembered. I speak in familiar ways so you will remember me
as well. This is the place for refuge, for letting go the body as the
exotic magnolias and kalmias do. Enter through the arbor covered
in rambling rector and you'll be washed of your worries—but do
not follow the stepping stones disappearing beneath the vines and
rock roses, for they will take you from me and are not meant for
visitation. Instead, trace the sweet briar and allium that border the
young Japanese maples; follow the honeysuckle on the thick trellis
just before the wide-arcing stone bridge your father built; follow the
geraniums and sage along the rolling plane of grass until an entrance
to the wood avails itself. You will find my soul there, still and
patient like night, having always been waiting for you to remember
me (I who am really you) as the dry earth remembers rain.

Victorian Garden

Come, come. This way to the house. Follow the folds of my path as they find their way through the rounds of shrubs along the fence, the bunches of lavender and tulips here and there. No, no, don't cut through the patch of lawn—let it be. Come sit by the pond beneath the oak, smell the clematis and honeysuckle as they mingle perfectly in the raised bed behind. Oh, do give me your impressions. We are so close to the house there's no need for secrets, to hold anything back—we are friends and confidents here, free as the wind and sunlight lifting up the kaleidoscope of cutting flowers, then the vast greens of vegetables by the kitchen door. I know that when you first came over this seemed much too usual, that perhaps you'd have passed by like you do the row houses up and down the street. But this is our sitting room, our front stoop, and don't the brilliant colors deep within call to you like the sunrise? Do you see the intricacies now? They are yours. Take what you want. By the iron gate there are climbing roses—feel free to pinch one off to lighten your dreary evenings at home. Do you remember what Shakespeare said? Will you come in then? Sit by the fire and have tea? Share stories and politics? Do you ever feel like you're not simply observing, but being observed as well?

Japanese Garden

Enter through the hedge like wind slipping from itself a stained earthly veil. Step forward with calm to find a stone in your path— all flowers open slow. Beside the tea house rinse your hands and mouth to show you walk from rivers. Speak softly in shade, smell cool dew against your feet, hear nothing but light. Yatsuhashi leads across calm water, trains stars beneath the surface. Beside a black pine one stone looks up, one over; something speaks inside. Waves of sand move still around three green islands, yet mountains cry within. Weeping willows trace the arc of my back like clouds—one leaf trembles. Lotus in the pond; we must rest here awhile like wonted stones. As the sky, gravel; as rivers, flesh of peony; without me, you.

Coneflowers, August

Monarchs fall upon the bulbous stamens,
give form to silent, passing origins

of place that two then three remember—they fuse
their rusty hues into the petals. No breeze

or passing drizzle from low autumn clouds
unfolds these watchful wings, clasped vertical

like paper hands in prayer—the dorsal fin
of faith carving through the darkened season.

Like finials they ride the stems, complete
designs beyond immediate perception.

But even the hushed roots of last year's growth
anticipate such endings as they push

apart the soil's mossy flesh in spring.
Until today the blooms were anything.

Suddenly, Autumn

Is it here at the window where we truly see
the brown-leafed oaks, the drying grass,
the bulge of clouds that darkens asphalt roads?

Is it within a frame of measured faith and chosen
color, relief of temperatures in flux—the southern
wind that fishtails from the north in thirty minutes,

sun spots glancing blows through tattered canopies?
How everything is almost everything we feel?
Loosening cold clothes from our tired limbs,

the quick friction warming us against the air,
then against ourselves, between our knees, our
arms and torsos, bone and streaming lungs.

Is morning like hot tea gripping at your chest,
flooding down and through you like some
revelation, incantation of the perfect pitch,

choral song of waking, sparrow, passing cars?
Will emptiness feel as bold, will the space
our body's voices leave be sacred words

that vision won't speak, that sound won't touch—
a place the mind can't frame without such absence?

Last Rites

Believe me when I say that lavender cries.
This is why in autumn mornings butterflies
move silently across the stalks, buoyant
like bells that slide over altar candles.
That exhalation, after scent has ambled
toward the heavens, removes life's memory, fervent
intensity of freedom from the stem—
it makes the world a stunted requiem.
And insects burning with the forests—wings
a folded canopy of maple red,
yellow ash, umber oak—these inclined
transmuted shadows slip into this wonting.
Even we, within our lightly tended beds,
will fade into another, intertwined.

Retirement—California, 1971

A shoreline. A couple. Older, probably
late sixties. Her hat, larger than the crane's
shadow that's caught in its blurred flight,
looks like a cargo ship against the cloud line.
Their heads are almost perfectly adrift
from their bodies, severed by the calm horizon.
His leg, the left, is naked to the knee,
his right is soaking wet up past his waist.
In the foreground: sand that's flat and hard,
compressed by tides that close upon themselves.
Threads of seaweed line a crab who's white
and spread eagle against the earth like stone.

The waves roll in, smooth as new bed sheets.
No matter the hour it seems clouds will burn
away before their lunch. It might be noon.
It could just as well be evening and the man
and woman set out to beat the rain, enjoy
the beach they'd come to settle toward. They've put
their dark shades on. They're wearing hats.
She's in a dress that shows her muscular calves.
But it's cold. It's fall. There's no one else nearby,
no ships across the water, and somewhere in front,
forty feet, a stranger stitches them against
horizons—ocean, sky, and land—the world
their bodies cross, but cannot navigate.

BENJAMIN VOGT was born in Oklahoma and grew up in Minnesota. He has a Ph.D. from the University of Nebraska-Lincoln and an M.F.A. from The Ohio State University. His work has been nominated for a Pushcart Prize and has appeared in *Diagram, Hayden's Ferry Review, Orion, Subtropics, The Sun,* and *Verse Daily.* He lives in Nebraska where he cultivates a native prairie garden.

www.ingramcontent.com/pod-product-compliance
Lightning Source LLC
LaVergne TN
LVHW092228200326
834410LV00020B/120